WHAT HAPPENS AT PELICAN PIER

Kids will sample sea-inspired, tasty, low-prep snacks and then dive right in to super-fun in science-based activities. We can't promise you'll stay dry, but we can be sure you'll know that God is with you wherever you go! Be sure to check out the gluten-free options provided for each session.

Here's what happens:

- Leaders review the daily theme.

- Kids assemble and eat a tasty, creative snack that ties in with the Bible story.

- Kids play a game or participate in a science activity that reinforces the daily theme.

- Discussion questions, conversation cues, prayers, and simple instructions help leaders talk with kids about God's presence in their lives and what it means to them.

SNACKS AND GAMES AT PELICAN PIER

Here's a quick look at the snack and game options for Deep Sea Discovery. Check them out, and choose the ones that work best for you!

	Session 1	Session 2	Session 3	Session 4	Session 5
SNACKS	Taste the Rainbow (GLUTEN FREE) Build a Boat	Gone Fishin' (GLUTEN FREE) Fruit Cup Fish (GLUTEN FREE)	Making Waves (GLUTEN FREE) Sink or Swim	Fruity Fish (GLUTEN FREE) Casting Nets	Float Your Boat (GLUTEN FREE) Traveler's Trail Mix
GAMES	Animal Rescue Drip, Drip, Drop Magic Bleach	What Do You Sea? "Spit Up" Relay Water Cannon	Toss Across Water Balloon Race Dive! Dive!	Hungry, Hungry Fishermen What a Catch! Down Periscope	Huff and Puff Dunk and Run Anchors Away!

Be sure to look over the anytime snacks and theme games for options that can be used for volunteer training, daily sessions, or for follow-up events!

GETTING TO KNOW PRETEEN KIDS

Everyone is different, of course. But as you interact with kids who visit your site, keep these things in mind:

Preteen kids . . .

- are developing at different rates and often feel awkward because of that.
- need activity and opportunities to move.
- are beginning to understand abstract and symbolic thinking.
- notice when people's words are different from their behavior.
- see themselves as young adults.
- can seem unbalanced due to internal and external physical changes.
- desire to have their opinions heard and respected.
- are highly sensitive to peer pressure.
- are receptive to God's offer of salvation.
- need caring, consistent adult role models to disciple them and help them grow in their faith.

Special Needs Tip: See the Elementary/PreTeen CD from the *Age-Level Resources Disc Set* for tips on teaching preteen kids with special needs.

GETTING TO KNOW ELEMENTARY KIDS

Everyone is different, of course. But as you interact with kids who visit your site, keep these things in mind:

Elementary kids . . .

• need to move.

• touch, handle, and explore everything.

• are eager to learn and ask a lot of questions.

• think in concrete terms, not abstract.

• are experiencing new and intense feelings.

• can have trouble controlling their behavior.

• like to have friends, but are still self-centered.

• love attention and will show off or act silly to get it.

• think prayer is important.

• think of Jesus as their friend.

• understand that they can choose right or wrong.

 **Special Needs Tip:** See the Elementary/PreTeen CD from the *Age-Level Resources Disc Set* for tips on teaching elementary kids with special needs.

LEADING KIDS TO CHRIST

One of the greatest joys of teaching is the opportunity to participate with kids as they begin thinking about salvation decisions. These suggestions will help you discuss salvation with them:

- **Use concrete terms.** Kids don't think abstractly. Use words that are accurate, comfortable, and appropriate.

- **Talk and listen.** Talking, questioning, thinking, and praying together will help you know a young person's desire and readiness for this important step.

- **Share with parents.** The best person to determine whether a child is ready to make a decision is the Christian parent.

- **Seek direction from the Holy Spirit.** He knows every kid's heart.

- **Share Bible verses.** Consider John 3:16; Acts 4:12; Acts 16:31-33; Romans 10:9, 13; Mark 16:16; Acts 2:36-38; Ephesians 2:8, 9; Revelation 2:10; Matthew 24:13.

- **Talk to kids individually.** Avoid situations in which peer pressure can influence this vital decision.

You will, of course, have kids in your program who don't come from Christian homes. As you nurture the faith of these kids, don't forget to include their parents as well.

WHY USE THESE SNACKS AND GAMES?

No one can argue the fact that cookies and kickball are the easy route. They're cheap. They're already prepared. And kids don't need any instruction. No argument there.

But just for a moment, think about what a little extra time, energy, and effort might inspire . . .

- **Natural talking and teaching opportunities.** The recommended snacks and games go right along with what kids are doing the rest of the day. Each includes conversation cues and discussion questions. No more awkward silences or random conversations about the weather. You'll know just what to say—and when to say it!

- **Prepare kids for or reinforce what they've already learned from the Bible story.** Whether kids see you or their Bible story leader first, what they learn and do during snacks and games ties into God's Word and the daily themes that teach kids that God KNOWS, HEARS, STRENGTHENS, LOVES, and SENDS them!

- **Help kids make natural applications between God's Word and their lives.** The open-ended questions you'll discuss lead kids to make their own discoveries about God. You're not reviewing facts or giving them the answers. Instead, you're guiding them on their journey to know and experience God on a personal level.

- **Remind kids that the Bible is relevant to everyday life, not separate.** By talking about God's Word and the daily focus at every site, kids will see it as more meaningful and real. What a gift to them!

- **Give kids many chances to process what they've heard.** As kids look at the same things from different angles and perspectives, they'll draw new conclusions. They'll think through what they've learned from God's Word, over and over, which will help them remember it longer.

Remembering God's Word . . . hiding it in their hearts . . . understanding that God loves them and is always with them–it doesn't get any better than that!

GETTING STARTED

As the snacks leader at Pelican Pier, you have the opportunity to interact with kids as they learn that God is with them wherever they go! Through the snacks you provide and the relationships that you nurture, kids will have a better understanding of God's love and presence in their lives.

Your responsibilities include:

- Praying for kids who will attend Deep Sea Discovery.
- Preparing a budget for snacks and supplies.
- Recruiting helpers.
- Choosing the snacks for each session.
- Calculating and collecting the food and supplies needed. (Go to www.vacationbibleschool.com and click on **Web Tools** for a handy snack calculator!)
- Checking registration forms for allergies. Do this every day, as new kids sign up.

QUICK TIPS FOR THE SNACKS LEADER

What you do at Pelican Pier is ultimately up to you. But here are some tips to keep in mind as you get started:

- Make samples of your snacks ahead of time. This will show kids what the end result will be and will help you anticipate any problems they may have.
- Calculate supplies and ingredients carefully to make sure you have enough. Always plan for more than you think you'll need.
- Cover tables and work areas with plastic cloths or roll paper. Have plenty of wet wipes handy for accidental spills or messes.
- Look carefully at the discussion suggestions and questions provided with each snack. What you say will drive home the same point kids are hearing throughout the session. Don't miss these important teaching moments.
- Call kids by name and make an effort to be sure everyone feels welcome and included.

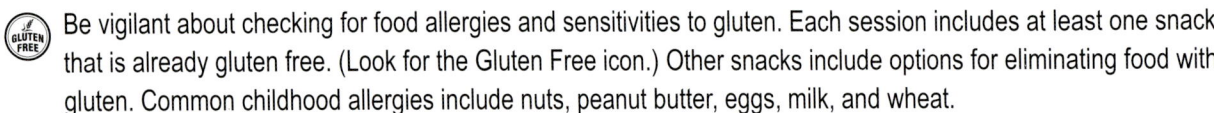 Be vigilant about checking for food allergies and sensitivities to gluten. Each session includes at least one snack that is already gluten free. (Look for the Gluten Free icon.) Other snacks include options for eliminating food with gluten. Common childhood allergies include nuts, peanut butter, eggs, milk, and wheat.

Special Needs Tip: Kids with special needs may be sensitive to certain textures and smells. We've provided tips throughout the materials, but you may want to ask a parent or caregiver if other adaptations will need to be made.

SNACKS

QUICK TIPS

DECORATING YOUR SNACKS AREA

Pelican Pier is hopping with the sights, sounds, and smells of the sea! Give your deep-sea explorers a fresh place to fuel up and breathe before they dive in for more discoveries!

Use these suggestions to set the tone for your snacks site:

- Paint scenes of colorful boardwalk shops on a sheet and hang on a clothesline as a backdrop.
- Use pool noodles to create nautical decor (see ideas on our Pinterest board or in the Decorating Guide).
- Use graphics from the Decorating & Publicity CD to add sea-themed art to your walls and tables.
- Use wood or cardboard to create pier arrow signs.
- Use pallet wood, cardboard, or brown paper and paint or markers to create a pier for the floor.
- Hang decorative fishnets on picnic tables or over blue tablecloths. Scatter seashells on the tables.
- Play sea sound effects in the background.

Consider special containers to serve snacks, such as:

- plastic sand buckets for utensils, napkins, or snacks
- wooden crates or trays
- round platters or trays inserted into lifesaver rings
- a clean baby pool or plastic sandbox filled with ice to serve as a cooler

Check out these products to make decorating simple and easy:

- *Deep Sea Photo Stand-up*
- *Site Name Poster Pack,*
- Decorating & Publicity CD
- *Decorating Resource Pack* with digital *Decorating Guide*

Check out the Standard Publishing VBS Pinterest boards and Facebook pages for tons of extra ideas and photos!

FUN FACTS ABOUT PELICAN SNACKS

As you spend time with kids who visit your site, share some of these facts about pelicans and how they eat!

- Pelicans eat fish, tadpoles, crustaceans, and even turtles. If they're *really* hungry, they might drown and swallow a seagull!

- Pelicans don't chew their food. After scooping up its prey, the pelican squeezes the water out the side of its bill, moves the food facing head-down in its throat, and then swallows it whole.

- Pelicans use their bills to sense creatures underwater. This way, if the water is too murky to see, they can still find something to munch on!

- Pelicans like to hunt in groups. They flap their wings on the water to send fish into shallow water, and then scoop them up with their bills.

- Pelicans have the most spacious beak of any bird in the world. A pelican can hold up to 3 buckets of fish in its mouth at once!

- A hook on a pelican's top jaw helps it grip slippery food. Sometimes pelicans use the hook to nab a large fish, toss it into the air, and swallow it in one gulp!

FISH STICKS

What You'll Need (for 1 serving)

2 pretzel rods
4 gummy fish
4 tbs blue frosting
$^1/_8$ tsp white pearl sprinkles
plastic knife
large paper plate

What You'll Do

Spread icing on the pretzel rods. Add gummy fish and sprinkles. As kids
create and eat their snacks, talk about how deep and amazing the sea is.
Remind them that God's love for them is even deeper and more amazing—and that He's with them wherever they go!

 **Special Needs Tip:** The white pearl sprinkles might be tough for kids with poor fine-motor control; allow
them to roll their pretzel in the sprinkles if that is easier. Be certain to model how you want kids to use the plastic
knives; kids with impulse-control difficulties may need reminders on how to be safe, even with plastic utensils!

SNACKS

ANYTIME SNACKS

TURTLE TREATS

What You'll Need (for 1 serving)

1 round slice of green apple

6 green grapes

black (or blue) gel frosting

$\frac{1}{8}$ cup lemon-lime soda

plastic knife

paper plate

To keep apple slices from browning, soak them in lemon-lime soda until ready to serve.

What You'll Do

Cut the grapes into halves and use them to create the legs, head, and shell of the turtle. Cut a small wedge to make a tail. Use gel frosting to add eyes. As kids create and eat their Turtle Treats, talk about how deep and amazing the sea is. Remind them that God's love for them is even deeper and more amazing—and that He's with them wherever they go!

PUFFER-FISH POPS

What You'll Need (for 1 serving)

1 cake pop covered in white chocolate
   and chilled

2 candy eyeballs

1 O-shaped piece of cereal

1 tsp white frosting

3–4 drops food coloring
   (color of choice)

plastic spoon

resealable plastic bag

scissors

Preparation

Cake pops need to be prepared and chilled ahead of time. Go online for recipes (or use donut holes!). You can add food coloring to the melted white chocolate, if you'd like.

What You'll Do

Spoon frosting into a resealable plastic bag. Add food coloring and seal. Knead with fingers to blend completely. Snip off one bottom corner of the bag and squeeze the frosting through the hole to make spikes on the puffer fish. Use additional frosting to attach candy eyeballs and a mouth. This snack is best done with a friend so that one person can hold the cake pop while the other person decorates. As kids create and eat their snacks, talk about how deep and amazing the sea is. Remind them that God's love for them is even deeper and more amazing—and that He's with them wherever they go!

JUICY JELLYFISH

What You'll Need (for 1 serving)

1 watermelon slice
1 piece string cheese
1 red grape
1 pineapple chunk

2 blueberries
2 banana slices
plastic knife
large paper plate

What You'll Do

Cut the red grape in half and pull string cheese apart into sections. Then use the ingredients to assemble the Juicy Jellyfish as pictured. As kids create and eat their snacks, talk about how deep and amazing the sea is. Remind them that God's love for them is even deeper and more amazing—and that He's with them wherever they go!

JELLYFISH JIGGLERS

What You'll Need (for 1 serving)

$1/3$ cup blue Jell-O
$1/3$ cup green Jell-O
$1/3$ cup whipped cream topping
clear plastic cup
plastic spoon

What You'll Do

Spoon blue Jell-O into a clear plastic cup. Add whipped cream topping, and then green Jell-O on top. As kids create and eat their snacks, talk about how deep and amazing the sea is. Remind them that God's love for them is even deeper and more amazing—and that He's with them wherever they go!

Option

If sugar and dye pose a problem for some kids, consider using green grapes and blueberries chopped up into small pieces. Bananas might work for the "foam" if kids can't have dairy.

FISH FOOD

What You'll Need (for 1 serving)

½ cup fish-shaped crackers
1 plastic bag
2 googly eyes
3 6" lengths of colorful ribbon (or string)
2" length of clear tape
plastic spoon
1" square colored paper (optional)

What You'll Do

Spoon crackers into the plastic bag, holding the bag at an angle so crackers settle in one corner. Twist the bag closed and secure with ribbons. (Cut small circles from colored paper, if desired, and then tape them to either side of the bag.) Add googly eyes. As kids open and eat their snacks, talk about how deep and amazing the sea is. Remind them that God's love for them is even deeper and more amazing—and that He's with them wherever they go!

💗 **Special Needs Tip:** Offer assistance to kids who might need help with the tying or with gluing on the eyes.

Option

For kids with gluten sensitivities, look for gluten-free treats to fill the bags instead.

DIVER'S DELIGHT

What You'll Need (for 1 serving)

1 cupcake (prepared, any flavor)
2 tbs blue frosting
1 tbs white frosting
1 fish-shaped cracker
2 round cereal pieces

3 large white pearl sprinkles
3" length of rope licorice
black gel frosting
plastic knife
paper plate

What You'll Do

Spread blue frosting on cupcake. Then spread white frosting in a small circle near the center. Add 2 pieces of cereal as pictured. Use gel frosting to outline the white area and to fill in the centers of the cereal pieces. Add white pearl sprinkles for bubbles and rope licorice as a snorkel. Place the fish-shaped cracker where desired. As kids create and eat their snacks, talk about how deep and amazing the sea is. Remind them that God's love for them is even deeper and more amazing—and that He's with them wherever they go!

SEAWATER SIPPER

What You'll Need (for 1 serving)

1 cup lemonade
1 ice cube
blue food coloring
clear plastic cup

What You'll Do

Prepare the ice cubes ahead of time, using food coloring to make them blue. Before serving, add an ice cube to a cup of lemonade. As kids enjoy their drinks, watch the lemonade change to look like seawater. Talk about how deep and amazing the sea is. Remind them that God's love for them is even deeper and more amazing—and that He's with them wherever they go!

TASTE THE RAINBOW

What You'll Need (for I serving)

4 strawberries

8 mandarin orange wedges

8 pineapple chunks

10 green grapes

15 blueberries

3 tbs whipped cream topping

plastic spoon

plastic knife

large paper plate

Preparation

Slice the strawberries into chunks ahead of time.

What You'll Do

1. Give each kid a paper plate and the ingredients listed. Help them assemble a rainbow as pictured, working from top to bottom. Spoon whipped cream topping along the bottom edge of the plate as clouds.

2. Let kids dip the fruit into the whipped cream topping as they eat.

What You'll Say

SAY: **What's today's Deep Sea Discovery?** (God KNOWS me and is with me!) **God placed a rainbow in the sky as a very special promise to Noah. God knew Noah was a good man. And God knows us too! He sees everything we do, and He loves us anyway. Let's thank Him for His love and for being with us wherever we go!**

PRAY: **Dear God, thank You for this food. Thank You for being with us and for loving us in spite of the wrong things we do. Help us to serve You by doing the right thing. In Jesus' name we pray. Amen.**

Option

If kids have dairy allergies, use bananas instead of whipped cream.

BUILD A BOAT

What You'll Need (for 1 serving)

4 pretzel sticks

3 chocolate animal crackers

1 ½ graham cracker squares

¼ cup fruit cereal

2 tbs blue frosting

plastic spoon

large paper plate

Preparation

Break graham cracker squares into individual pieces as shown.

What You'll Do

1. Give each kid a paper plate and a plastic spoon. Distribute ingredients and help them assemble the snack as pictured. Start with the ark, and then add the animals and the rainbow. Finish by spooning blue frosting along the bottom of the plate as water.

2. Kids can dip their food in the frosting as they eat.

What You'll Say

SAY: **What's today's Deep Sea Discovery?** (God KNOWS me and is with me!) **God used an ark to save Noah and his family. God knew Noah was a good man. And God knows us too! He sees everything we do, and He loves us anyway. Let's thank Him for His love and for being with us wherever we go!**

PRAY: **Dear God, thank You for this food. Thank You for being with us and for loving us in spite of the wrong things we do. Help us to serve You by doing the right thing. In Jesus' name we pray. Amen.**

Option

Use gluten-free crackers, pretzels, and cereal for kids with food sensitivities.

GONE FISHIN'

What You'll Need (for 1 serving)

1 banana
2 vanilla (or lemon) wafers
2 mini chocolate chips
¼ cup yogurt fruit dip

blue food coloring
plastic spoon
plastic knife
large paper plate

Preparation

Use blue food coloring to color the fruit dip.

What You'll Do

1. Give each kid a paper plate and a plastic spoon. Dip fruit dip onto the center of each plate. Peel the banana and remove about 2" from one end. Cut a small slit in the other end.

2. Break or cut the wafers in half. Insert 1 half into the slit cut in the end of the banana. Insert 2 other halves into the sides as fins. Add chocolate chips as eyes.

What You'll Say

SAY: **What's today's Deep Sea Discovery?** (God HEARS me and is with me!) **God used a huge fish to save Jonah. Even inside that fish, God heard Jonah. And God hears us too! God answers our prayers because He loves us. Let's thank Him for His love and for being with us wherever we go!**

PRAY: **Dear God, thank You for this food. Thank You for being with us and for caring enough about us to listen when we pray. Help us to serve You by praying for others. In Jesus' name we pray. Amen.**

Option

Use blue Jell-O in place of the fruit dip. You can also make this a gluten-free snack by using gluten-free wafers.

FRUIT CUP FISH

What You'll Need (for 1 serving)

1 packaged fruit cup
1 colored index card
scissors
permanent markers
clear tape
plastic spoon

♥ **Special Needs Tip:** Use fresh fruit if necessary to reduce sugar intake or eliminate food dyes (often in maraschino cherries).

What You'll Do

1. Give each kid a fruit cup, an index card, and a pair of scissors. Help kids cut 3 triangles from the index card to make fins and a tail as pictured. Use tape to attach the pieces to the fruit cup.

2. Let kids use permanent markers to draw faces and scales on their fruit cups. Then distribute spoons and help kids open the cups as needed.

What You'll Say

SAY: **What's today's Deep Sea Discovery?** (God HEARS me and is with me!) **God used a huge fish to save Jonah. Even inside that fish, God heard Jonah. And God hears us too! God answers our prayers because He loves us. Let's thank Him for His love and for being with us wherever we go!**

PRAY: **Dear God, thank You for this food. Thank You for being with us and for caring enough about us to listen when we pray. Help us to serve You by praying for others. In Jesus' name we pray. Amen.**

MAKING WAVES

What You'll Need (for I serving)

2 gluten-free graham cracker squares
2 gummy bears
4 tbs blue frosting
plastic knife
paper plate

What You'll Do

1. Give each kid a paper plate, a plastic knife, and
   2 graham cracker squares. Have kids spread blue
   frosting on graham crackers, using the tip of the
   knife to make waves.

2. Let kids add gummy bears on 1 cracker before eating.

What You'll Say

SAY: **What's today's Deep Sea Discovery?** (God STRENGTHENS me and is with me!) **Jesus gave Peter strength when Peter was afraid. And God strengthens us too! God helps us do hard things that we can't do on our own. Let's thank Him for His love and for being with us wherever we go!**

PRAY: **Dear God, thank You for this food. Thank You for being with us and for helping us to do things that aren't always easy. Help us to serve You by encouraging others. In Jesus' name we pray. Amen.**

Option

Use regular graham crackers in place of gluten-free if gluten sensitivities aren't a problem. If children have dairy allergies, consider using the gummy bears and graham crackers only, and allow kids to "sail" the rafts over a bed of cotton balls or blue crepe paper.

SINK OR SWIM

What You'll Need (for 1 serving)

1 cup blue Jell-O®
2 bear-shaped graham crackers
2 tsp whipped cream topping
blue food coloring
plastic spoon

What You'll Do

1. Give each kid a Jell-O cup and a spoon. Have kids put the whipped cream topping on their Jell-O. Add a drop or two of blue food coloring and let kids stir the whipped cream to make waves.

2. Add graham cracker bears (or gummy bears) to the Jell-O before eating.

What You'll Say

SAY: **What's today's Deep Sea Discovery?** (God STRENGTHENS me and is with me!) **Jesus gave Peter strength when Peter was afraid. And God strengthens us too! God helps us do hard things that we can't do on our own. Let's thank Him for His love and for being with us wherever we go!**

PRAY: **Dear God, thank You for this food. Thank You for being with us and for helping us to do things that aren't always easy. Help us to serve you by encouraging others. In Jesus' name we pray. Amen.**

Option

Make this a gluten-free snack by substituting gummy bears for bear-shaped crackers. Use bananas as "foam" if students are allergic to dairy.

FRUITY FISH  GLUTEN FREE

What You'll Need (for 1 serving)

3 blueberries
1 green apple wedge
½ strawberry
1 clementine

1 candy eyeball
plastic knife
paper plate

Preparation

Save time by peeling the clementines prior to the session.

What You'll Do

1. Give each kid a paper plate, a plastic knife, and a clementine. Have kids break the clementine into 2 halves and lay 1 half in the center of the plate as the fish's body. Use the remaining sections of the clementine to make fins and a tail.

2. Let kids cut triangles from the apple wedge to make grass. Use the tip of the strawberry to make a mouth. Add blueberries as bubbles and a candy eyeball before eating.

What You'll Say

SAY: **What's today's Deep Sea Discovery?** (God LOVES me and is with me!) **Jesus loved His disciples so much that He wanted them to understand who He is and why He came to earth. And He loves us too—enough to die on a cross! Let's thank Him for His love and for being with us wherever we go!**

PRAY: **Dear God, thank You for this food. Thank You for being with us and for dying to save us. Help us to serve You by sharing Your love with others. In Jesus' name we pray. Amen.**

CASTING NETS

What You'll Need (for 1 serving)

10–15 pretzel squares
10–15 fish-shaped crackers
5 tsp chocolate hazelnut spread
plastic knife
paper plate

What You'll Do

1. Give each kid a paper plate, a plastic knife, pretzels, and crackers. Spoon chocolate hazelnut spread onto each plate.

2. Have kids use a knife to spread chocolate hazelnut spread on their pretzels. They can add a cracker to the top of each pretzel before eating.

What You'll Say

SAY: **What's today's Deep Sea Discovery?** (God LOVES me and is with me!) **Jesus performed a miracle with fish and nets to help His disciples understand who He is and why He came to earth. Jesus loved His disciples and He loves us too—enough to die on a cross! Let's thank Him for His love and for being with us wherever we go!**

PRAY: **Dear God, thank You for this food. Thank You for being with us and for dying to save us. Help us to serve You by sharing Your love with others. In Jesus' name we pray. Amen.**

FLOAT YOUR BOAT

What You'll Need (for 1 serving)

4 apple wedges

8 cheese cubes

4 fruit picks (or toothpicks)

large paper plate

$\frac{1}{8}$ cup lemon-lime soda

bowl

4 tbs caramel dip (optional)

Preparation

To keep apples from browning, soak them in lemon-lime soda until ready to serve.

What You'll Do

1. Give kids a plate and 4 fruit picks.

2. Let kids put cheese cubes on fruit picks as pictured. Attach the fruit picks to apple wedges as pictured.

What You'll Say

SAY: **What's today's Deep Sea Discovery?** (God SENDS me and is with me!) **God had a special mission for Paul—to spread the good news of Jesus around the world. And God sends us too! Let's thank Him for His love and for being with us wherever we go!**

PRAY: **Dear God, thank You for this food. Thank You for being with us and for giving each of us special talents and gifts. Help us to serve You by telling Your story in the best way we can. In Jesus' name we pray. Amen.**

Option

Serve with caramel dip. For kids with dairy allergies, replace cheese with cantaloupe.

(♥) Special Needs Tip: Demonstrate how children should use the fruit picks, and allow them to practice.

TRAVELER'S TRAIL MIX

What You'll Need (for 1 serving)

5–10 cheese puffs
¼ cup Chex® cereal
¼ cup fish-shaped pretzels
¼ cup fish-shaped crackers
clear plastic cup
plastic spoon

What You'll Do

1. Give each kid a plastic cup and spoon.

2. Let kids make their own trail mix using the ingredients provided.

What You'll Say

SAY: **What's today's Deep Sea Discovery?** (God SENDS me and is with me!) **God had a special mission for Paul—to spread the good news of Jesus around the world. And God sends us too! Let's thank Him for His love and for being with us wherever we go!**

PRAY: **Dear God, thank You for this food. Thank You for being with us and for giving each of us special talents and gifts. Help us to share Your love by telling Your story in the best way we can. In Jesus' name we pray. Amen.**

Option

Use gluten-free crackers, pretzels, and cereal. Add dried fruit and chocolate candies.

GETTING STARTED

As the games leader at Pelican Pier, you have the opportunity to interact with kids as they learn that God is with them wherever they go! Through the games you play and the relationships that you nurture, kids will have a better understanding of God's love and presence in their lives.

Your responsibilities include:

- Praying for kids who will attend Deep Sea Discovery.
- Preparing a budget for games and supplies.
- Recruiting helpers.
- Choosing the games for each session.
- Collecting the supplies needed.
- Taking safety precautions and making backup plans for outdoor games, in the event of inclement weather.

QUICK TIPS FOR THE GAMES LEADER

What you do at Pelican Pier is ultimately up to you. But here are some tips to keep in mind as you get started:

- Play the games ahead of time. This will ensure that you explain things well, and will help you anticipate any confusion kids may have.

- Calculate supplies carefully to make sure you have enough. Always plan for more than you think you'll need.

- Have a first-aid kit and plenty of drinks handy, just in case!

- Look carefully at the discussion suggestions and questions provided with each game. What you say will drive home the same point kids are hearing throughout the session. Don't miss these important teaching moments.

- Be an example of good sportsmanship. Make sure kids and volunteers respect the rules of each game, but keep things lighthearted and fun!

- Call kids by name and be sure everyone feels welcome and included.

♥ Special Needs Tip: Kids with special needs may prefer another option or many simply need alternatives to some of these games. We've provided tips throughout the materials, but you may want to ask a parent or caregiver if other changes will need to be made. See the Elementary & PreTeen CD in the *Age-Level Resources Disc Set* for additional suggestions.

DECORATING YOUR GAMES AREA

Pelican Pier is hopping with the sights, sounds, and smells of the sea! Give your deep-sea explorers a place to stretch their sea legs as they splash and learn together!

Use these suggestions to set the tone for your games site:
- Paint scenes of colorful boardwalk shops on a sheet and hang on a clothesline as a backdrop.
- Use pool noodles to create nautical decor (see ideas on our Pinterest board or in the Decorating Guide).
- Print out diving markers or flags from the Decorating & Publicity CD and attach them to string to hang a pennant garland.
- Use wood or cardboard and colorful paint to create pier arrow signs.

Consider having extra games on hand for kids to enjoy, such as:
- water guns in a tub of water
- pool noodles and DIY sponge balls for a game of soggy softball
- area marked out for games of Sharks and Minnows
- water balloons, launchers, and targets to make a water balloon shooting range

Check out these products to make decorating simple and easy:
- *Deep Sea Photo Stand-up*
- *God Is with Wall Me Banner*
- *Site Name Poster Pack*
- Decorating & Publicity CD
- *Decorating Resource Pack* with digital *Decorating Guide*

You'll also want to check out the Standard Publishing VBS Pinterest boards and Facebook pages for tons of extra ideas and photos!

FUN FACTS ABOUT PELICAN GAMES

As you spend time with kids who visit your site, share some of these fun facts about how pelicans move and play!

- Pelicans can soar at heights of 10,000 feet on gigantic wingspans as large as 10 feet.

- There are 8 living species of pelicans on earth, and they can be found on every continent except Antarctica.

- Pelicans are some of the heaviest flying birds. They have air sacs in their bones and in the skin on their throat, chest, and wings. The air sacs are connected to their lungs and fill with air to give them extra buoyancy.

- The air sacs in a pelican's chest and wings also cushion the impact when the birds dive into the water for fish.

- When pelicans are courting, they strut around, open and close their bills, and toss sticks and dried fish up into the air to show off for the opposite sex. Their bills and pouches also change color to attract a mate.

- Both male and female pelicans help to keep their eggs warm by standing on them with their webbed feet.

SPONGE TAG

What You'll Need

large playing area
bucket of water
large sponge (or several, depending on number of kids)

What You'll Do

1. Play this game like a normal game of tag, except that the person who is "It" must tag other kids by throwing a wet sponge. Once "It" has hit someone with the sponge, that person must grab the sponge, run back to the bucket, and dip the sponge in water before tagging someone else.
2. Play as time allows. Then talk with kids about how all the Bible stories at Deep Sea Discovery involve water. Talk about how God was with the people they've been learning about and how He is with each of them—wherever they go!

Option

If playing space is limited, have kids tag each other by touching other players with the sponge rather than throwing it. If you have a large group, add extra sponges and kids to be "It."

(♥) **Special Needs Tip:** As with most water activities, kids with sensory sensitivities may not want to participate. Consider offering a "dry sponge" game as well as a wet sponge one so everyone can play. Model how the game works so that kids who struggle with impulse control can play respectfully.

WATER BALLOON SPOON RACE

What You'll Need

small balloons filled with water (1 per person)
wooden spoons (1 for every 6–8 kids)
bowls (1 for every 6–8 kids)
parking cones

Preparation

Use cones to mark off a starting line in your playing
area. Place another cone about 20' away. Put 5 balloons
in each bowl and place them along the starting line.

What You'll Do

1. Divide kids into groups of 6–8. Have each group line up behind the starting line, next to a bowl. Give the first person in each group a spoon.
2. At your signal, the first person in each group will place a water balloon on the spoon and walk around the cone in the center of your playing area. The first person back to the starting line with a balloon intact is the winner.
3. Repeat the race with kids who are next in line. Play until everyone has a turn. Then talk with kids about how all the Bible stories at Deep Sea Discovery involve water. Talk about how God was with the people they've been learning about and how He is with each of them—wherever they go!

WHAT DID YOU SEE?

What You'll Need

cookie sheet

dish towel

25 small items of various kinds (toy block, keychain, rubber band,
bottle cap, lip balm, toothpick, piece of candy, pen cap, etc.)

paper and pencil for each person

Preparation

Spread out all the items on the cookie sheet and cover it completely with a towel.

What You'll Do

1. Give each person a piece of paper and a pencil. Have everyone gather around your covered cookie sheet.
2. Remove the towel for 30 seconds. During that time, have kids look at the items and try to remember as many of the items as possible. Replace the towel.
3. Have kids write down as many of the items as they can remember. Review the items together to see who was the most accurate. Play again as time allows. Talk with them about how God sees and notices and loves each one of them. He's with them wherever they go!

 **Special Needs Tip:** Consider assigning Diving Buddies to serve as "writers" so kids who struggle with spelling/writing can participate without worry!

TRACK IT DOWN

What You'll Need

prepared list of items
paper and pen to tally scores
additional helpers

Preparation

Prepare a list of items for kids to track down, such as: flip-flop, yellow sock, pair of glasses, belt, hair clip, braces, freckles, bracelet, long brown hair, white shoelaces, the color pink, the number 12, etc.

What You'll Do

1. Divide kids into groups of 8–10. Give each group a number, and assign a helper to each group. As you call out each item from your list, groups will work together to find the item within their own group and bring it back to show a helper (being sure to tell them which group number they are). Helpers will tally how many items each group finds.
2. After you've worked through the list, see which group collected the most items. Talk with kids about how God sees and notices and loves each one of them. He's always looking out for them, and He's with them wherever they go!

Options

This game can also be played outdoors, which will allow for a broader variety of things for kids to find. You could also give each group a copy of the list and let them gather things to return to the helper all at once.

LEARN IT, POP IT! BIBLE MEMORY

What You'll Need

balloons (2 per word from the Bible Memory of your choice)
permanent marker

Preparation

Inflate the balloons, and write 1 word of the verse each on a separate
balloon. Repeat with remaining balloons so that you have 2 sets of the
verse. Mix up the balloons and place them in a central spot. For outdoor fun, fill the balloons with water instead of air.

What You'll Do

1. Divide kids into two groups. At your signal, the first person in each group will go to the balloons, find the first word, and bring that balloon back to the group. The second person will find the second word, and so on. When all the words to the verse have been collected, have kids in each group hold the balloons and stand in order. After saying the verse together correctly, have them sit on each balloon (in order) to pop it. The first team to finish is the winner.
2. Afterward, talk to kids about how they might use the verse in everyday life and to name times when it might be especially helpful.

(▶) **Special Needs Tip:** Be aware that some kids will be afraid of the balloon popping sounds. Warn them when this is about to happen, and allow them to cover their ears or watch from a distance.

GO DEEP! BIBLE MEMORY

What You'll Need

foam football
8 ½" x 11" sheets of card stock
  (1 per word or group
  of words from the Bible Memory
  of your choice)

marker
clothesline
clothespins (2 per sheet
  of card stock)

Preparation

Hang a clothesline in your playing area, allowing plenty of room in front of and behind it. Write each word (or phrase) of the verse on a sheet of card stock. Use clothespins to hang the cards on the clothesline (in order).

What You'll Do

1. Stand behind the clothesline and use the football as a pointer, holding it over each card as kids read the words. After you review the verse, throw the football to one of the kids, who will take your spot and do the same thing. That person will then throw the ball to another kid, and the process continues. Encourage kids to get faster and faster with each round. If time allows, play again, this time mixing up the order of the cards.
2. Afterward, talk to kids about what the Bible verse means. Ask them how they might use the verse in everyday life and to name times when it might be especially helpful. Then have the entire group review the verse together one last time.

ANIMAL RESCUE

What You'll Need

plastic animal figures (about 10 per group of 5)
buckets (1 per group of 5)
masking tape

Preparation

Use the masking tape to make one long line.
Place the buckets about 6' away.

What You'll Do

1. Divide kids into groups of 5. Have groups line up behind the stationary line, and give each group the same number of plastic animal figures. Designate a bucket for each group.
2. At your signal, the first person in each group tosses one animal into the bucket. If he misses, he retrieves the animal and hands it to the next person in line. If he makes it, he goes to the end of the line and the next person tries to toss another animal into the bucket.
3. The first group to get all its animals into the bucket wins. Groups may need to cycle through a few times in order for all animals to make it into the bucket.

What You'll Say

SAY: **What's today's Deep Sea Discovery?** (God KNOWS me and is with me!) **God used a man named Noah to save a whole ark full of animals—and God saved Noah because God knew that Noah loved Him. And God knows us too!** ASK:

- Why did God choose Noah to build the ark?
- God knew that Noah loved Him and would follow His instructions. What types of things does God know about you?
- God knows all about you and still loves you just the same. How can you show God that you love Him too?

Option (additional materials are needed)

Make the game more interesting by placing each bucket on a brick (or small stool) inside a kiddie pool filled with water. The animals will then fall into the water if they don't make it inside the bucket.

 **Special Needs Tip:** Some students with motor-planning difficulties might struggle with this game; offer an option to those kids to be an "Ark Captain" and report on the success of each toss. Or, provide a couple of different lines from which kids can toss, and allow them to choose. Demonstrate that some animals will go in and others will not . . . it just takes practice! Also demonstrate what to do/say when an animal does NOT go into the bucket. Sometimes this can prevent meltdowns because kids will have the language to express disappointment and encouragement.

DRIP, DRIP, DROP

What You'll Need

bucket with water (1 per group of 10)
large sponge (1 per group of 10)

Preparation

Place buckets at least 20' apart to allow plenty of room for kids to run.

What You'll Do

1. Divide kids into groups of 10. Have each group sit in a circle around a bucket.
2. One person will dip the sponge into the bucket of water and walk around the outside of the circle. This game is similar to Duck, Duck, Goose in that the person with the sponge will hold the sponge over her teammates' heads as she walks, saying "Drip" each time she passes someone. When she chooses, she will wring out the sponge over a teammate's head and call out "Drop!" The seated student will get up and chase her around the circle and back to the empty spot. If the student with the sponge gets there first, the other person gets the sponge and the game restarts. If the seated student wins the race, the person with the sponge sits in the middle of the circle and loses one turn.
3. Let groups play as time allows. Encourage groups to make sure everyone has a chance to get wet (if they want to!) before giving anyone else a second turn with the sponge.

What You'll Say

SAY: **What's today's Deep Sea Discovery?** (God KNOWS me and is with me!) **God sent rain for 40 days to flood the earth. But God kept Noah safe and dry because God knew Noah loved Him. And God knows us too!** ASK:

- **Why did God choose Noah to build the ark?**
- **God knew that Noah loved Him and would follow His instructions. What types of things does God know about you?**
- **God knows all about you and still loves you just the same. How can you show God that you love Him too?**

Option

Encourage kids to learn each other's names by adding a twist to the game. Rather than calling out "Drop!" when they wring out the sponge, kids must yell out the person's name. If they get it right, the race is on. If not, players switch roles and play resumes.

(♥) **Special Needs Tip:** Let kids choose whether or not they'd like to get wet. Consider having some extra T-shirts on hand for those who get very soggy and wish to change into dry clothes.

MAGIC BLEACH

What You'll Need

2 identical clear glasses
pitcher of water
bleach

red food coloring
spoon (or stir stick)

Preparation

You'll need to experiment with exact proportions of food coloring and bleach. Practice a few times prior to doing the demonstration for the kids so that it will be as effective as possible. Place about 1" of liquid bleach in the bottom of one of the glasses before kids arrive.

What You'll Do

1. Gather kids in close and begin the demonstration. Tell kids that God created the earth to be pure and spotless. (Fill the empty glass ¾ full of water.)
2. Explain that, over time, people did many wrong things and sin came into God's perfect world. (Add a few drops of food coloring to the glass of water and stir.)
3. Tell kids that God chose a man named Noah to help with a plan to start again. God sent rain for 40 days to wash away the bad things in the world and make everything new. (Pour the red solution into the glass containing the bleach. Stir until the red solution disappears. This will take 60 seconds or so. As you stir, explain that God has a plan for us to start again too. He sent Jesus to the cross so that all our sins would disappear, just like red stains in

the water. And when we choose to follow Him, we get a brand-new life too!)

4. Be very careful when handling bleach products. The resulting clear liquid will not be safe to drink.

What You'll Say

SAY: **What's today's Deep Sea Discovery?** (God KNOWS me and is with me!) **God knew Noah loved Him, and so God used Noah in a very special way. And God knows us too!** ASK:

- **Was Noah a perfect person?** (No, only Jesus never sinned.)

- **Are you a perfect person?**

- **How do you feel, knowing God loves you in spite of the wrong things you do?**

- **How can you show God that you love Him too?**

Option

If you have adult helpers, set up different stations where kids can get more closely involved with this demonstration. Have each helper do the activity, assigning jobs to kids in their group (e.g., pouring water, adding food coloring, stirring the water).

♥ **Special Needs Tip:** Be VERY cautious that kids don't try to drink the liquid. Some students who struggle to control impulses or who have other special needs try to put non-food items in their mouths frequently. When a liquid looks like water or a juice drink, it might be even more difficult for them to resist.

WHAT DO YOU SEA?

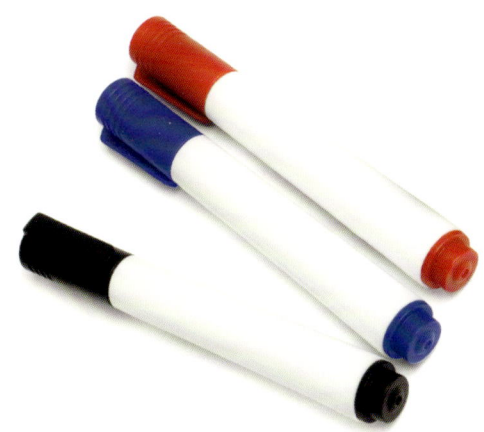

What You'll Need

large whiteboard
2 dry-erase markers
index cards
pen
timer

Preparation

Before kids arrive, write on separate index cards various items or animals that might be found at the bottom of the sea. Be creative! (Examples: octopus, fork, shark, crate, tire, oar, shell, bottle, eel, etc.)

What You'll Do

1. Divide kids into two equal groups. Have each group choose one person to come to the board and draw. Give each of those kids a marker, and then show them what is written on one of the cards. Explain that they will be drawing things that can be found at the bottom of the sea.
2. At your signal, both kids will begin drawing what you've written on the card. Both groups will guess what's being drawn, and will raise their hands when they have a guess. You decide whose hand went up first and who first guesses correctly.
3. When a group makes a correct guess, they get a point. Choose different kids to come up front and draw, using a new card. Continue guessing and giving points as time allows.

What You'll Say

SAY: **What's today's Deep Sea Discovery?** (God HEARS me and is with me!) **A man named Jonah spent some time at the bottom of the sea, praying to God. God heard Jonah's prayers and answered them! And God hears us too!** ASK:

- **What are some other things you might see at the bottom of the sea?**
- **Why do you think God takes the time to hear your prayers?**
- **If God was with Jonah at the bottom of the sea, is there any place where God isn't with you?**

 **Special Needs Tip:** Drawing can be very difficult for some kids with disabilities. As an alternative, provide some verbal cues during the drawing to help kids guess correctly. Invite kids to choose whether or not they want to draw.

"SPIT UP" RELAY

What You'll Need

2 buckets full of water
2 men's XL T-shirts
2 cones

Preparation

Set up your relay by placing a cone for each team at one end of the playing field and a bucket of water for each team at the other end.

What You'll Do

1. Divide kids into 2 equal groups. Have groups line up behind the cones. Give the first person in each line a T-shirt.
2. At your signal, the first person in each group takes the T-shirt and runs to his team's bucket of water. He then dunks the T-shirt completely in water and puts it on. Once the shirt is on, he yells, "Ewww—I've been spit up!" and runs back to his group. After tagging the cone, he removes the T-shirt and hands it to the next person in line, who then repeats the process.
3. The first group to complete the task is the winner.

What You'll Say

SAY: **What's today's Deep Sea Discovery?** (God HEARS me and is with me!) **A man named Jonah was swallowed by a giant fish! Jonah prayed to God, and the fish spit Jonah out. God heard Jonah's prayers and answered them! And God hears us too!** ASK:

- **What do you think it would be like inside a fish?**
- **If God heard Jonah inside a fish, is there any place where God can't hear you?**
- **What do you think Jonah said to God after the fish spit him out?**

Option

If you'd prefer a game that won't get kids drenched, set up an obstacle course with sprinklers, water guns, etc. Kids can run through the course and yell, "Ewww—I've been spit up!" as they exit.

(♥) **Special Needs Tip:** Kids with sensory issues may struggle to enjoy this relay. Offer a choice so that they may watch or participate. As an alternative, find a refrigerator box or other large appliance box and have kids help to decorate it so it looks like a fish on the outside (use precut "scales" from construction paper, etc.). Then allow them to take turns feeling what it might be like inside the fish, and acting out what it would be like to be "spit out."

WATER CANNON

What You'll Need

hot glue gun
plastic soda bottle (22 oz)
medium-size balloon
duct tape
water

Preparation

Use a hot glue gun to melt a small hole in the lower ⅓ of the soda bottle.
Practice this activity ahead of time so you are comfortable with it.

What You'll Do

1. Place the neck of the balloon tightly and completely over the mouth of
   the bottle. Stuff the rest of the balloon inside the bottle.
2. Leaving the hole in the bottle uncovered, blow up the balloon inside the bottle. Keeping the balloon inflated, place a
   piece of tape over the hole in the side of the bottle. This will equalize the air pressure, and the balloon should stay
   inflated. If air leaks between the bottle and the balloon, the balloon will deflate.
3. Pour water into the inflated balloon. Aim the bottle away from kids (unless you want them to get wet) and remove
   the tape. The water should go spewing out.

What You'll Say

SAY: **What's today's Deep Sea Discovery?** (God HEARS me and is with me!) **A man named Jonah was inside a giant fish for three days! Jonah prayed to God, and the fish spit Jonah out. God heard Jonah's prayers and answered them! And God hears us too!** ASK:

- What do you think it would be like to be spit out of a fish?
- If God heard Jonah inside a fish, is there any place where God can't hear you?
- What do you think Jonah said to God after the fish spit him out?

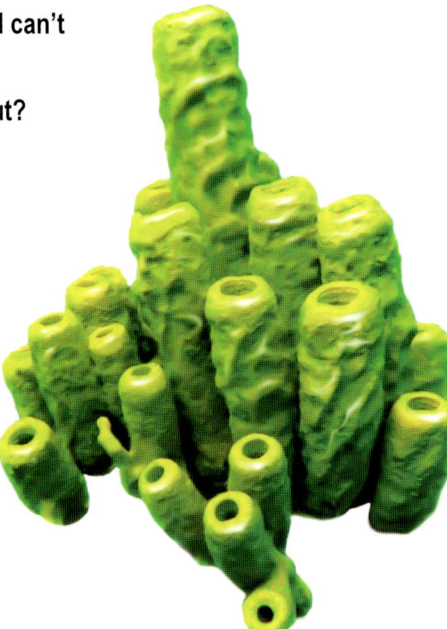

TOSS ACROSS

What You'll Need

12-muffin muffin tins (1 for every group of 6–8 kids)
water
ping-pong balls (several per group)
coins (1 per group)
parking cone

Preparation

Fill each cup in the muffin tins with about 1" of water. Randomly place a coin in one cup of each tin. Place the tins in a line, leaving about 3–4' in between. Use the cone to mark a line about 5' away from the tins.

What You'll Do

1. Divide kids into groups of 6–8. Refer to the muffin tins and show that one cup in each contains a coin. That's the cup they will be aiming for.
2. Give each group several ping-pong balls. At your signal, kids will take turns trying to toss the balls into the cups containing the coins. A player should toss the balls until she lands a ball in the cup with the coin or until she runs out of balls. She should then go retrieve the balls and hand them to the next person in line.
3. If you'd like, establish a point system (5 points for the cup with the coin and 1 point for the other cups). Play for a designated amount of time, and then declare a winning team.

What You'll Say

SAY: **What's today's Deep Sea Discovery?** (God STRENGTHENS me and is with me!) **Jesus had 12 disciples, but only one of them walked to Jesus on the water. And when that disciple got scared and began to sink, God strengthened him! And God strengthens us too!** ASK:

- Have you ever felt like you were sinking—not in water, but in life?
- When has God helped you do something that was hard or scary?
- When have you helped someone else do something that was hard or scary?

WATER BALLOON RACE

What You'll Need

large (or medium) balloons (1 for every 2 kids)
water
2 parking cones
laundry baskets (or trash bags)

Preparation

Fill balloons with water and tie closed. Place them in a basket until you're ready to use them. Place cones in your playing area, about 20' apart.

What You'll Do

1. Group kids in pairs. Have them stand back-to-back and link arms.
2. Have pairs line up near the starting cone. Place a water balloon between the backs of the first pair in each group. At your signal, pairs will race (arms linked, balloon between their backs) around the far cone and back.
3. Chances are, many of the balloons will burst. When that happens, the pair is out of the race and should go back to cheer on the remaining pairs. If the balloon doesn't burst, the pair returns to the end of the line and gets to try again.

What You'll Say

SAY: **What's today's Deep Sea Discovery?** (God STRENGTHENS me and is with me!) **It felt pretty awkward to walk with a balloon between you and your partner. But can you imagine what it would feel like to walk on water? Peter did! And when he got scared and began to sink, God strengthened him! And God strengthens us too!** ASK:

- Have you ever felt like you were sinking—not in water, but in life?

- When has God helped you do something that was hard or scary?

- When have you helped someone else do something that was hard or scary?

DIVE! DIVE!

What You'll Need

plastic 2-liter bottles with lids (1 per pair of kids; remove wrappers)
packets of ketchup (or soy sauce) (1 packet per pair)
water
bowl

Preparation

Fill the bottles nearly to the top, leaving 5" or so of air. Put lids on bottles. Test the
packets of ketchup to find those that contain at least some air pockets. To do so, place each packet
in a bowl of water, and discard those that sink to the bottom. (Since soy sauce packets are see-through, you can tell
merely by looking whether they contain any air.) Practice this activity ahead of time so you are comfortable with it.

What You'll Do

1. Divide kids into pairs. Give each pair a bottle of water and a packet of ketchup.
2. Have kids remove the lids from the bottles and carefully place their packets inside. Have them work together to twist the lids on as tightly as possible.
3. Let kids take turns squeezing their bottles and observing what happens. When the air inside the bottle is compressed (squeezed), the packets should sink.

What You'll Say

SAY: **What's today's Deep Sea Discovery?** (God STRENGTHENS me and is with me!) **Peter bravely walked to Jesus on the water. But when he felt the pressure of what was going on around him, Peter got scared and began to sink. God strengthened him! And God strengthens us too!** ASK:

- Have you ever felt like you were sinking—not in water, but in life?
- When has God helped you do something that was hard or scary?
- When have you helped someone else do something that was hard or scary?

HUNGRY, HUNGRY FISHERMEN

What You'll Need

large, open playing area
100 inflated balloons (or plastic balls)
4 plastic laundry baskets
4 skateboards
4 lengths of rope (or bungee cord)
4 bike helmets

Preparation

Place the balloons in the center of the playing area. Place a laundry basket, skateboard, length of rope, and a bike helmet in each corner. This game is a TON of fun, but you may want to have some extra helpers to make sure it's played safely.

What You'll Do

1. Divide kids into 4 teams. Place each team in a corner. Have one person on each team put on the helmet and lie facedown on the skateboard. Loosely tie one end of the rope to one of his ankles, and give him a laundry basket (which he should hold upside down).
2. At your signal, team members will push the person on the skateboard out into the playing area, where he will use the basket to trap as many balloons as he can in the spot where he is. Team members will then use the rope to pull

him back to the corner where he started. He then gives the helmet, skateboard, and basket to the next person, who then repeats the challenge.

3. When all the balloons have been collected, the team with the most balloons in its corner is declared the winner.

What You'll Say

SAY: **What's today's Deep Sea Discovery?** (God LOVES me and is with me!) **Jesus performed a miracle and gave His friends more fish than their nets could hold! Jesus LOVED His disciples, and He loves us too!** ASK:

- **Why is it important to love other people the way that Jesus did?**
- **When is it hard to love others?**
- **How can you share God's love with someone today?**

 **Special Needs Tip:** Kids with motor issues or low muscle tone will have a great deal of difficulty with this game. As you prepare for the activity, assess the needs and strengths of the kids in the group. Determine how everyone can participate in a fun and meaningful way. Consider modifying the activity so that kids can play without the skateboard, or work with their Diving Buddies.

WHAT A CATCH!

What You'll Need

large tug-of-war rope
3 bandannas
water sprinkler with hose

Preparation

Tie 1 bandanna in the center of the rope. Tie the other bandannas about 10' from each end. Lay the center of the rope across the water sprinkler. (If you have a very large group, set up more than 1 game.)

What You'll Do

1. Divide kids into 2 equal teams. Have each team line up at opposite ends of the rope, behind the bandannas.
2. At your signal, both teams will pull on the rope as hard as they can.
3. The team that pulls the other team across the sprinkler in the center is the winner. Play again as time allows.

What You'll Say

SAY: **What's today's Deep Sea Discovery?** (God LOVES me and is with me!) **Jesus performed a miracle and gave His friends more fish than they could pull in! Jesus LOVED His disciples, and He loves us too!** ASK:

- **Why is it important to love other people the way that Jesus did?**
- **When is it hard to love others?**
- **How can you share God's love with someone today?**

Option

If you don't have access to a water sprinkler, lay a blue tarp on the ground and pretend it's water.

♥ **Special Needs Tip:** Tug-of-war games are so much fun, but can get out of control. Some kids might overtake those with poor muscle control or weakness. In addition, students are very close to each other, which can be hard for some kids with special needs. Be extremely careful when doing this activity so that kids remain safe. An alternative would be to have kids work together to "reel in" an object with the rope.

DOWN PERISCOPE

What You'll Need

kiddie pool
water
bubble bath
see-through shower cap
aluminum coffee can (no lid)

can opener
electrical tape
small, heavy items to hide under the bubbles (coins, keys, small objects that will sink)

Preparation

Add bubble bath as you fill the pool with 8–10" of water. Completely cover the surface of the water with bubbles. Place the small, heavy items in the pool, around the perimeter. Use a can opener to remove the bottom of the coffee can, and then use electrical tape to seal the shower cap onto one end of the can. Stretch the cap tightly, and be sure no water can leak between the can and the shower cap.

What You'll Do

1. Show kids how to kneel down and place the "periscope" into the water to see below the surface. As the can is gently pushed into the water, the bubbles are forced out of the way so that the items below the surface are revealed.
2. Let all kids take a turn looking beneath the bubbles and finding the hidden items.

What You'll Say

SAY: **What's today's Deep Sea Discovery?** (God LOVES me and is with me!) **Even though we can't see Him, God is always with us and He loves us!** ASK:

- **When are some times when it doesn't feel like God is with you?**
- **How does it feel to know God loves you and is always with you?**
- **How can you share God's love with someone today?**

Option

Make several periscopes, and have kids count the number of items on the bottom of the pool. The one whose guess is the most accurate is the winner. Or have kids race to search for a certain item.

♥ **Special Needs Tip:** Be sure to have some specific rules about how students should behave around the water (water stays in the pool, hands stay out of the pool, etc.). This will help with impulse control and also protect kids who have sensory sensitivities from being splashed!

HUFF AND PUFF

What You'll Need

ping-pong balls (1 for every 6–8 kids)
painter's tape (use rope if you're outdoors)

Preparation

Use painter's tape to create aisles about 2' wide and 10' long. Make an aisle for every 6–8 kids. Also mark a clear beginning and end to each aisle, which will serve as start and finish lines.

What You'll Do

1. Divide kids into groups of 6–8. Give each group a ping-pong ball and designate an aisle for each group. Have groups line up behind each starting line.
2. At your signal, the first person in each group will kneel and race to blow his team's ping-pong ball from the starting line to the finish line. Once there, he picks up the ball and races to give it to the next person in the group.
3. Kids must keep the ball in their aisle. If the ball crosses the tape, kids must return to the starting line and begin again.
4. The first group to have every member complete the challenge is the winner.

What You'll Say

SAY: **What's today's Deep Sea Discovery?** (God SENDS me and is with me!) **In Bible times, boats were powered by oars or by sails. The wind would blow into the sails to make the boats move. God sent Paul on a boat to tell His story, and God sends us too!** ASK:

- Have you ever been on a boat? What was it like?
- Why is it important for us to go and share God's story with everyone?
- How can you share God's story with someone today?

Special Needs Tip: For kids who have difficulty with breath support or gross-motor coordination, this activity could be challenging. If they need to start again each time the ball strays out of the lane, frustration could result. Consider allowing kids to work with Diving Buddies, or to have the option of observing or cheering for team-mates if they are worried about their ability to participate. Another option would be to limit the amount of times they need to start over (e.g., after two start-overs, they can hand off to the next person).

DUNK AND RUN

What You'll Need

bucket (1 per group of 6–8)
water
aluminum pie tins (2 per group of 6–8)
crispy rice cereal (2 cups per group of 6–8)
parking cones

Preparation

Use cones to mark out a relay zone at least 25' long. Fill buckets with water and place
1 for each group at a designated starting line. Place pie tins with cereal midway through
the relay zone. Place empty pie tins at the far end of the relay zone.

What You'll Do

1. Divide kids into groups of 6–8. Have each group line up behind a bucket of water. Designate a pie tin with cereal and an empty pie tin for each group.
2. At your signal, the first person in each group will dunk his face in the bucket of water and run to the pie tin with cereal. With his hands behind his back, he should put his face into the cereal and try to get as much of it stuck to his face as possible. He then runs to the empty pie tin and uses his hands to scrape the cereal from his face into the tin.
3. When the first player has finished, the next person in each group repeats the challenge.
4. The group with the most cereal in the last pie tin at the end of the race is the winner.

What You'll Say

SAY: **What's today's Deep Sea Discovery?** (God SENDS me and is with me!) **Your mission in this game was to get as much cereal on your face and into the tin as possible. This was a pretty silly mission, but God has an important mission for you! God sent Paul on a boat to tell His story, and God sends us too!** ASK:

- How do you think Paul felt when the church sent him to preach about Jesus?
- Why is it important for us to share God's story with everyone?
- How can you share God's story with someone today?

 **Special Needs Tip:** This activity will be fun to do or to watch. Kids with anxiety or sensory sensitivities might not want to participate in this, but will probably enjoy watching. Offer a variety of jobs (e.g., cheerleaders, pan holders, cereal pourers, etc.) so that everyone can participate.

ANCHORS AWAY!

What You'll Need

cookie sheet
aluminum foil
scissors
toothpicks
liquid dish soap
water

Preparation

Use scissors to cut a small square (less than 3") of aluminum foil. Fold the foil like a paper airplane, creating a point at one side. Cut a small, deep rectangle into the boat, opposite the point. The resulting shape should look like a house with a tall door. (See photo.) Fill a cookie sheet with just enough water to cover the bottom. Practice this activity ahead of time so you are comfortable with it.

What You'll Do

1. Place your boat at one end of the cookie sheet.
2. With a toothpick, place a single drop of liquid dish soap into the open rectangle of your boat. Watch as the boat zips across the water to the other side of the cookie sheet.

What You'll Say

SAY: **What's today's Deep Sea Discovery?** (God SENDS me and is with me!) **In Bible times, boats were powered by oars or by sails. The wind would blow into the sails to make the boats move. God sent Paul on a boat to tell His story, and God sends us too!** ASK:

- Have you ever been on a boat? What was it like?
- Why is it important for us to go and share God's story with everyone?
- How can you share God's story with someone today?